SAFETY FIRST

Hazards And Safety At Places

VICTOR CHINAZA OKEREKE

ISBN-13: 9798394460203
ISBN-10: 1477123456

Cover design by: Art Painter
Library of Congress Control Number: 2018675309
Printed in the United States of America

CONTENTS

INTRODUCTION

This is a detailed field exposure textbook of Health, Safety and Environment (HSE) which will provide the user the opportunity to identify hazards and mitigate them at workplaces. It is intended for use by everyone.

This volume covers several aspects in Health, Safety and Environment at workplace, Safety Signs/Symbols, HSE Communication, Safety Rules and Standards, Hazards and Mitigations, Injuries, Near Misses, Employer and Employee Rights, HSE/OSHA Policies/Standards etc.

This is largely due to my vast experience in the labour sector for quite a considerable number of years with academic qualification and professional certifications from reputable institutions. All these are with the view to improving and sharpening the safety awareness of the user through bringing a real world experience into this book.

CHAPTER 1

HEALTH, SAFETY AND ENVIRONMENT (HSE)
Safety and Hazards At Workplaces

1.1 Concept of HSE Awareness At Workplace

An ideal workplace is an environment in which a worker is or feels safe and able to maximize his/her productivity, therefore the idea of raising awareness of hazards and safety at workplaces is to adequately equip workers with all necessary approaches/tools to mitigate the rising hazards/dangers and achieve safety in workplaces. Although many of these occupational hazards are specific to a particular discipline.

The objective of HSE is to eradicate or mitigate as low as possible the practicable causes of loss due to incidents and accidents, along with its associated costs.

HEALTH (H): this relates to the physical condition of both body and mind of every human being at the workplace and their protection from harm in the form of injury or disease.

Occupational Health is the promotion and maintenance of the highest degree of physical, mental and social wellbeing of workers in all occupations by preventing departure from good health, controlling risk and adaptation of work to people and people to work. Occupational Health is concerned fundamentally with two aspects:

1. The relationship of work to health

2. The effect of work upon the worker

SAFETY (S): this relates to the condition at the workplace and applies to the pursuit of a state where the risk of harm has been eliminated or reduced to an acceptable level. Safety is concerned with identifying Hazards, Risks and Threats with the aim of planning and implementing control and barriers for bringing the accident causal factors to a low level.

ENVIRONMENT (E): environmental protection is concerned with the protection and the preservation of life and natural resources in the environment, this includes:

The Workplace Environment which refers to the general condition in the immediate area of the workplace itself: noise, light exposure, temperature, heat etc.

The External Environment refers to pollution to the air, land, water and living creatures outside of the workplace if they might be affected by workplace activities.

1.2   Safety   Consciousness   And   HSE Communication

Safety consciousness is not applicable to the engineering profession alone, it cuts across a nursing mother, a carpenter, a teacher, a driver, a pastor, a kiosk operator etc., irrespective of the industry that you are in, safety should always be your priority before you carry out any task. Not observing/ adhering to safety measures can cost your life, the lives of your loved ones, staff or others, it can as well result to life threatening illnesses or permanent loss of parts of the body or loss of properties worth millions of money. As a professional, if you will be working with electricity/electrical gadget, chemicals, fire, moving/rotary equipment, heights, depths, wild animals/ pets, dangerous/extreme working conditions, unsafe weather, etc. you must understand basic safety measures before and while working. As an ordinary person look within your environment, you will observe sharp objects, obstructions, near misses or hazards everywhere. If you are less concerned about safety, it's totally wrong because somebody or properties might be affected negatively. For safety reasons, remove the hazards, sharp objects and obstructions to prevent accident. Take precautionary measures that will avoid injury to lives and properties. While working in the office, house, cooking, travelling, etc. there are always hazardous situations that will always present themselves. If you are not conscious of hazards in your environment and the impending threats associated with the hazardous substances present, injuries, loss of lives and properties might occur. **Always remember that injuries, death**

and loss of properties occur due to human actions or inactions. Therefore, safety depends on human preventive actions.

HSE Communication: this is important in the regulation of risks and management of hazards in the workplace. It allows people to participate in or be effectively represented in decisions about managing risks. It helps in putting decisions into practice, helps people to understand regulations, informing and advising people about risks and how to control, dissuading them from unsafe and risky behaviour. HSE Communication can be achieved through:

Signs/Symbols/Signage: these are combination of shape, colour and pictorial symbols to give specific HSE information or instructions in accordance to widely accepted standards.

Posters and Stickers: these are very important tool in HSE communication in work or public places where there are hazards. These can help communicants directly discuss and pass on vital information which will assist in safe work.

Reports and Statistics: Statistics and Reports are results of the performance of the safety management system in a workplace. It shows the effectiveness of the system as well as giving room for accurate measurement of performance.

Newsletter and Bulletin: newsletters are designed and published for a particular reason while Bulletin are posted on boards, sometimes as adverts to communicate with people and the outside world.

Safety Signs and Meanings

These are combination of shape, colour and pictorial symbols to give specific HSE information or instructions in accordance to widely accepted standards. These standards are recognized globally regardless of language.

Categories of Safety Signs

A. PROHIBITION SIGN:

These signs are circular with RED as the main colour, with a black symbol on white background and diagonal cross bar. Intended to stop dangerous action/behaviors: No smoking, trespassing, naked fire.

B. MANDATORY ACTION

These signs are circular with BLUE as the main colour, with a white symbol. Instructing people to carry out action/behaviors usually relating to wearing personal protective equipment (PPE): safety helmet, shoes, gloves must be worn.

C. WARNING SIGN:

These signs are triangular with YELLOW as the main colour, with a black symbol and black border. Instructing people to be careful and take precaution to a particular hazard:

Electric shock, radiation, slippery surface, forklift in operation.

D. SAFE CONDITIONS:

These signs are rectangular with GREEN as the main colour, with a white symbol on green background. Intended to identify safe behaviour or place of safety

E. FIRE-FIGHTING EQUIPMENT:

These signs are rectangular with RED as the main colour, with a black symbol on red background. Intended to identify particular types of equipment and locations: fire extinguisher, labels and hose reel instructions

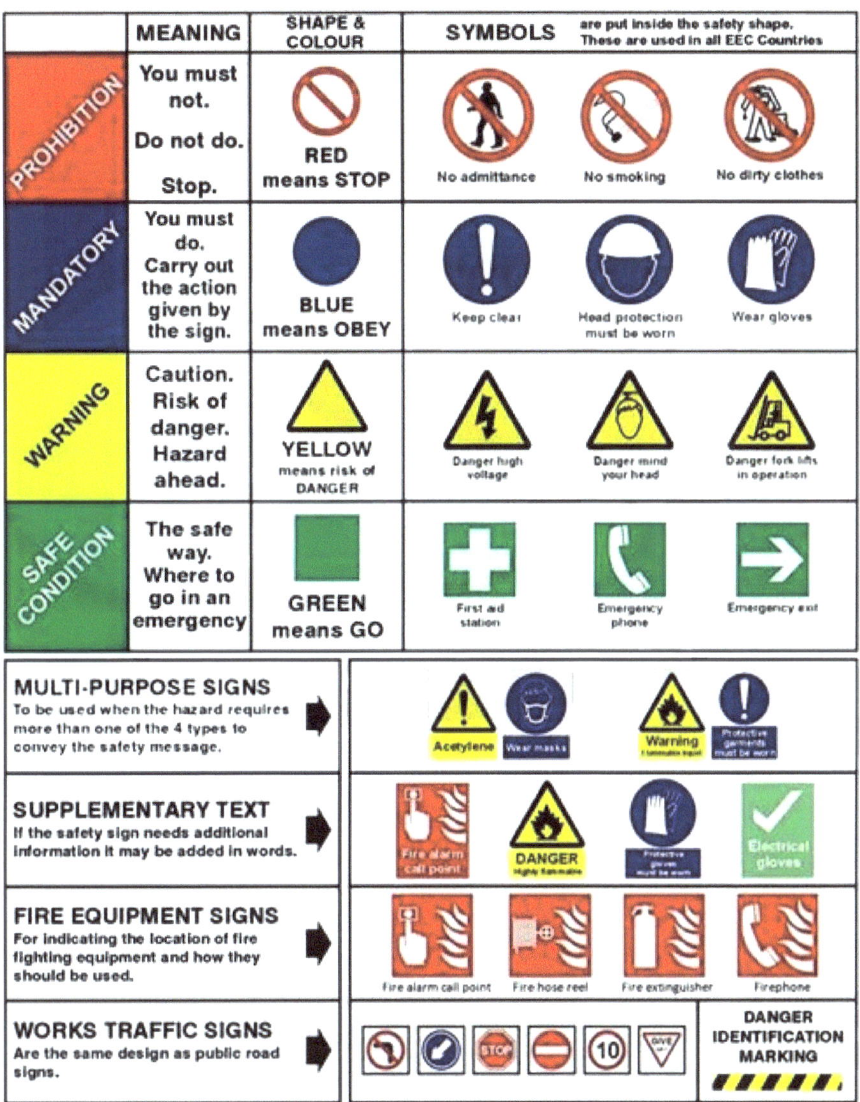

1.3 Safety Triangle

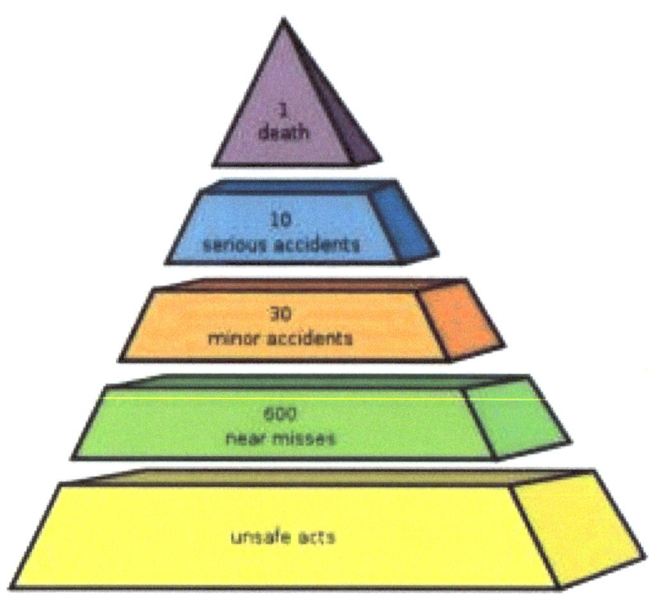

The safety triangle (Safety Pyramid, Heinrich's Triangle, Bird's Triangle) was propounded by Heinrich and it's an imaginary model that explains the ratio between workplace happenings (hazards) of varying degree of severity.

Traditionally, the ratio of the safety triangle is given as 1 – 10 – 30 – 600 which denotes 1 serious injury (leading to fatality, disability, time wasted or professional medical treatment) for every 10 minor injuries (requiring first aid), every 30 accidents (resulting in property damage), and every 600 safety incidents. Before a particular hazard happens, there should have been a corresponding hazard of lesser severity.

That means for you to have one hazard resulting in one serious injury, there should have been 10 minor injuries, 30 accidents resulting in property damage and 600 safety incidents. Accepting this premise implies that we should always work from the bottom of the **safety triangle** because the same behaviour that leads to near-misses will eventually lead to serious injuries. Safety triangle helps inform us that effective hazard controls and safety training is key to accident reduction in our workplace. In general, each industry has its specific safety measures and standard already put in place, compliance to such safety measures is mandatory for the safety of lives and properties. Personal Protective Equipment (PPE) such as safety shoes, safety helmets, reflecting jackets, gloves, safety belt, full body harnesses with permanent lifeline should be strictly mandatory for all workers and all jobs

NOTE:

> Never work on energized circuits or perform duties that you are not qualified for.

> Never be nervous while working, always be very calm and cut off all forms of distraction

> Don't stretch or overload electrical cables. Minimize the use or damaged or joined cables

> Avoid contact with expose wires that are not insulated

> Physical barriers must always be install close to hazardous electrical locations. Ensure that cabinet doors on electrical panels are always close.

> If you are working in an area where an electrical hazard is present, always assume that electrical parts are live, and act accordingly. Do not use conductive tools in the area.

> If you are cleaning any electrical circuit, note that some cleaning materials are conductive as well and require additional caution. Solvent and water-based cleaning materials are electrically conductive, keep these cleaning products, as well as any conductive tools, away from live electrical parts and equipment.

1.4 Workplace Culture

Employers, employees and customers have an obligation to work together to create a safety culture. This holds true for all sectors as employers must consider the safety of their employees, employees must consider the safety of the customers. Many companies have stringent safety protocols and policies to mitigate workplace accidents which includes:

1. Physical Accidents which could result in injury, disability and death

2. Operational Accidents which includes repairs and replacement of equipment, implication of public image and regulatory repercussions.

3. Financial Accidents which could lower operational effectiveness or production.

Safety at all levels and sectors of any organization is integral to personal well-being and operational effectiveness therefore organizations must make safety a priority and create an atmosphere that places emphasis on safety and make sure all employee are involved. Also employers/companies should develop safety and health programs, policies and procedures along with conducting routine observations and scrutiny. Employers should keep records, make sure to resolve safety and health issues in a timely manner and inform workers of their right and responsibility.

Employers should ensure compliance with HSE standards and regulations, they should provide employees with the trainings, tools, and equipment needed to perform work responsibilities safely. Employers should consider the following threats:

High risk work environment

High risk facility and equipment

Toxic and flammable products and by-product

Working at dangerous height, above/beneath water.

Working under adverse condition; noise, weather, stress etc.

Working with complex processes.

1.5 Reinforcing Effective Workplace Safety

1. Leadership: for great leadership there should be Awareness, Commitment and Incentives.

Awareness: consist of safety committees, safety posters and bulletin boards.

Commitment: consists of management and employee involvement.

Incentives: consists of rewards for safety performance and maintaining safe work practices.

2. Actions: to maintain consistent action, there must be effective hazard preventions and controls which involves worksite hazard analysis, toolbox, safety meetings and daily job site briefing.

3. Education: to achieve maximum workplace safety, there must be effective safety and health trainings, conventions of safety rules, standards and procedures to make employee constantly aware of conditions in work areas that can produce injuries as no employee is required to work at a job where he/she is not safe.

Employees must know that company management is fully committed to safety therefore complying with established policies and procedures endorses the commitment to safety. Management must ensure that all employees adhere to the company's safety policies and procedures without exceptions.

CHAPTER 2

CATEGORIES OF WORKPLACE HAZARDS

2.1 Categories of Workplace Hazards

1. Work Organization Hazards: this includes other organizational job activities, prolonged work hours and duties causing stress, injuries or death to a worker if not checked

2. Physical Hazards: this involves high noise pitches, extreme temperature, and extreme radiation, pressure causing injuries or death to a worker.

3. Biological Hazards: this includes insect, pets, molds, communicable diseases and infections a worker is exposed to that causes injuries or death

4. Chemical and Dust Hazards: this includes poisonous substance, dusts, chemicals, cleaning products, asbestos, pesticides causing injuries or death to a worker if not prevented

5. Ergonomic Hazards: this includes awkward positions, lifting, postures, screen light and repetition actions causing injuries or death to a worker if not controlled

6. Safety Hazards: this involves faulty equipment, trips, falls, and slips causing injuries or death to a worker.

Electrical hazards (Arcing, sparking, overheating, friction, static electricity, electrical current leakage fault) are one of the most common causes of fires and thermal burns in the workplace, coming in contact with electrical voltage can cause current to flow through component or your body resulting in fire, explosion, electrical shock, burns, serious injuries or death. Electrical shock occurs when a human body completes the current path between two energized conductors in an electric circuit or between an energized conductor and a grounded surface or object. Therefore, it is imperative that employees are conscientious while recognizing possible hazards, evaluating and controlling them, special precautions and more protocols must be followed as employee work on equipment and systems that carry electrical power.

There are other types of hazards that can cause injuries/accident if not prevented theses includes:

1. Working at dangerous height/depth (poles, towers and pits)

2. Handling a hazardous substances (poisonous chemicals, reactive/radioactive materials, flammable and combustible liquids, corrosive materials, compressed/poisonous gases, etc.)

3. Working with a moving/rotating machine or a machine with high pitch of dangerous decibels,

4. Working as a driver, fire fighter, computer operator, etc.

Employees have the right to know how hazardous the equipment/substance they are handling, therefore a Material Safety Data Sheet (MSDS) must be provided. It contains information about equipment/substances such as toxicity, usage, storage, handling and emergency procedures. It explains what to do when accident occurs and how to recognize symptoms of overexposure to safeguard workers and reduce injuries, illnesses, deaths and fires caused by use of hazardous materials.

2.2 Workplace Injuries And Symptoms

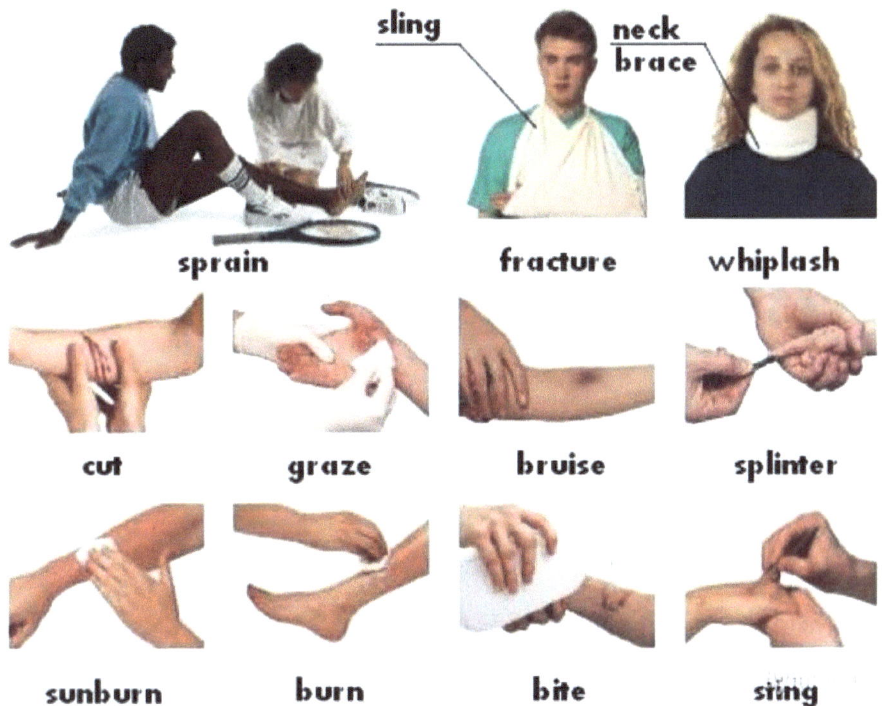

Several employers have policies in place regarding injuries, safety and first aid treatment. Keep in mind that in some accident cases, no treatment except by medical personnel is the best immediate treatment. During a hazardous potential electrical power work, workers are subject to more stringent first aid requirements, in such scenario two people are require as a crew so that one can provide first aid to the other person if needed. Generally, when accident involving electric shock occurs, first de-energize the power line so that emergency medical personnel can provide treatments to victims.

2.3 Causes of Electrical Hazard

Bad wiring: Having a wrong electrical power installation

Exposed components: contacting uncovered components with electrical power

Power lines: Touching naked electrical cables carrying electricity

Poor insulation: Using poor and fake insulation materials

Improper grounding: Contacting an equipment/building with faulty grounding

Overload: Operating an equipment/machine beyond its rated capacity

Wet conditions: Contacting an electricity conducting liquids or working under rain in a thunder region.

Faulty Tool/Equipment: Working with a faulty tool or equipment that conducts electricity to the user

Improper use of Personal Protective Equipment (PPE): Inappropriate use of PPE while working on electricity or electrical machines.

Levels of Electrical shock:

The severity of electrical shock depends on several factors which includes: body resistance, circuit voltage, amount of current flowing through the body, the current path through the body, area of contact and duration of contact.

At 1milli Amp: tingling sensation

Greater than 3milli Amp: itchy sensation

At 5milli Amp: biting sensation

Greater than 10milli Amp: shock

At 30milli Amp: shock

Greater than 50milli Amp: shock and burn

At 100milli Amp and above: shock, heart arrest or death

2.4 First Aid Kit and Contents

A small box containing items such as bandages, plasters, antiseptics wipes etc. for use while giving help to a sick or injured person until a full medical treatment is available. Several HSE compliant organizations and employers have medical first aid kit visibly/accessibly placed in locations in case of injuries.

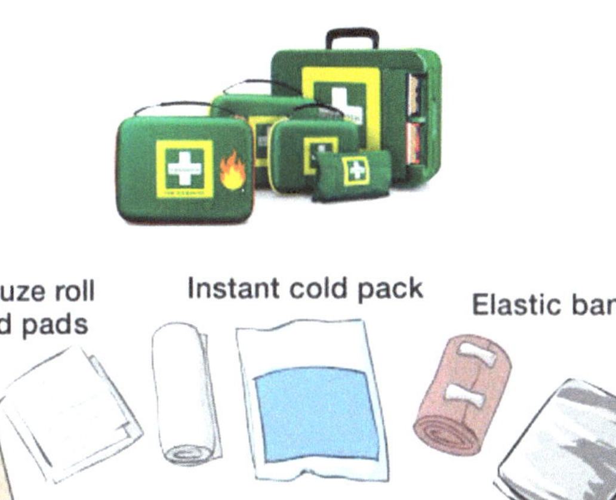

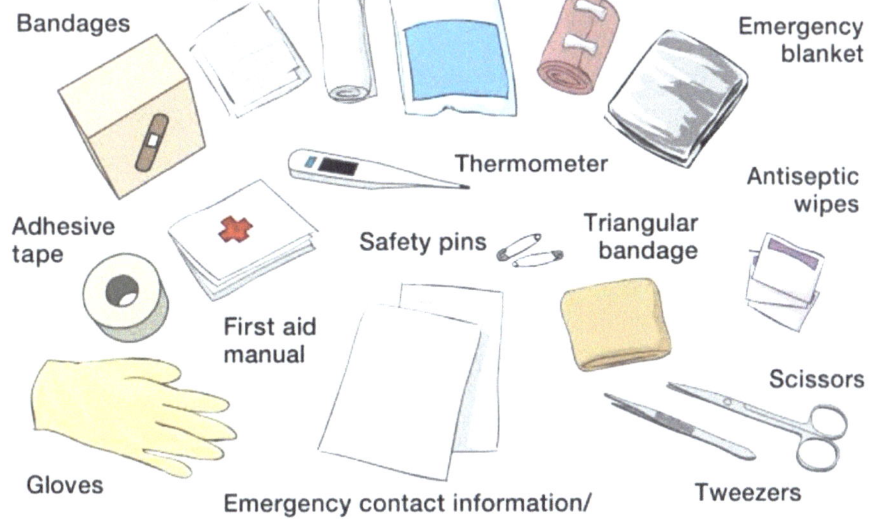

2.5 Kinds of Injuries at Workplaces and Treatments

Cuts: Easily identified and non-emergency unless the cut is very deep and bleeding heavily. Wash with soap and water or wiping with an alcohol swab and then apply antibiotics ointment and bandage, transport victim to hospital if bleeding doesn't stop.

Stings: Insect sting generally raises a red wealth at the site, allergic workers may experience Anaphylaxis (swollen throat) and difficulty in breathing. Sting is non-emergency but Anaphylaxis is an emergency and immediate medical treatment is required. Treat insect stings with Antihistamine cream or Epinephrine or Epipen for allergic workers to prevent death.

Bites: Aggressive animal bites may result in tearing or breaking the skin, workers need training to avoid being bitten. Medical attention is needed for detoxification and stitches. Small scrapes, tears and punctures should be treated by washing with soap, water and apply bandage. Antibiotics is required to prevent infection.

Broken Bones and Dislocation: Broken bones are difficult to identify unless it is a compound fracture while dislocation result in swollen joint. An x-ray is required to confirm the bone condition. Do not move a victim with broken bone, keep watch on the victim and make sure of breathing, you may apply ice to reduce swelling while waiting for emergency experts.

Spinal Injury: A victim with spinal injury may experience numbness, pain or no immediate symptoms and requires emergency care by professionals. Do not move or reposition the victim and if unconscious don't attempt to awaken the victim by shaking the shoulders. Keep the victim's head immobile by placing a pillow or towel on either sides and keep the airways clear. Monitor the breathing and call for emergency.

Thermal Burns: Thermal burns caused by heat or fire are categorized by their severity as:

1st Degree burn which is non-emergency but superficial injuring the outmost layer of skin and causing redness and pain like sunburn and scalding. Keep the skin under cool water not ice water to stop the burn, if it subsides keep the burn clean and dry. Don't apply butter, ointment or bandage.

2nd Degree burn causes blisters as well as redness and may cause pain unless nerve endings are destroyed. If 2nd degree burn covers a large area of the body, its an emergency and medical treatment is required.

3rd Degree burn destroys all the three layers of the skin, skin appears white or charred and victim may not feel pain or sensation because the nerve endings are burned, this is an emergency requiring immediate medical attention. Exposure to electric current (electrocution) may cause electrical burns with same characteristics with thermal burns. Use and wear an insulated material to de-energize the line and remove the victim from the power source. Do not risk electrical burns, shocks or electrocution to yourself trying to save a victim.

Chemical Burns: Chemical burns are caused by skin exposure to corrosive chemicals, these burns must be washed immediately though blisters may form. Remove the clothing soaked with the spilled chemical. In most cases, washing with water continuously if appropriate will dilute the chemical and result in further skin damage due to type of chemical. If burn is large and extensive medical treatment is required.

Electric Shocks: Cases of electric shock, amount of electric power and length of exposure determines the effects. Exposure to a large amount of electric power may cause muscle contractions, heart Arrhythmias or may throw the victim some distance from the source while exposure to small amount of current create only a tingling sensation. This serious conditions are an emergency and requires immediate medical attention. Use and wear an insulated material to de-energize the line and remove the victim from the power source. Do not risk electrical burns, shocks or electrocution to yourself trying to save a victim.

Shock: This is a physical response that occurs in response to an accident, symptoms are pale skin, rapid pulse, increase breath rate, weakness, nausea, cold hands and clammy skin which can result to death. Immediate emergency treatment is required. Do not reposition the body if there are broken bones, spinal or head injuries serious enough to warn a victim's body going into a shock merit emergency call. Keep the victim calm by assuring medical personnel is coming and call for medical treatment. Remember WART to prevent possible shock. W (warmth) keep the victim off damp ground and cover with blanket if needed. A (Airways, unobstructed Breathing, Circulated pulse) of the victim should be checked, R (Reassure and Rest) speak calmly to the victim, keep the victim relatively still and from anxiety, T (Treatment) treat the injury.

Heart Attack: Symptoms of heart attack usually start with mild discomfort or chest pain, often mistaken for indigestion and grow more painful. In addition of feeling heavy pressure or squeezing underneath the breastbone, victims may experience shortness of breath, nausea, sweating and vomiting. Treat all severe chest pain as though it is a heart attack, immediate medical attention is needed. Call emergency, ask the victim a question and listen for response, watch the chest to see if the victim is breathing, if not breathing but has pulse, begin artificial respiration. If no breathing and pulse then the victim is in cardiac arrest, call for medical treatment.

Stroke: Signs of a stroke are numbness, paralysis particularly on one side of the body, speech disturbance. Loss of balance, confusion, vision trouble and severe headaches. A quick check for stroke involves asking the victim to raise both arms, smile and repeat a simple sentence and inability to do these indicates stroke in progress and immediate medical attention is needed. Call emergency, ask the victim a question and listen for response, watch the chest to see if the victim is breathing. If no breathing and pulse then the victim is in cardiac arrest, call for medical treatment.

Unconsciousness: Unconscious person will be unresponsive and may or may not be breathing, this may be the result of an injury, drug, alcohol use or illness such as diabetes. This is a medical emergency and immediate treatment is required. Call emergency, ask the victim a question and listen for response, watch the chest to see if the victim is breathing, if not breathing but has pulse, begin artificial respiration. If no breathing and pulse then the victim is in cardiac arrest, call for medical treatment. If accident occurs in a workplace, you shouldn't be a helpless bystander, since doing nothing can potentially worsen the situation. Have proper first aid knowledge and provide quick medical treatment until medical professional arrives.

2.6 Classes of Fire

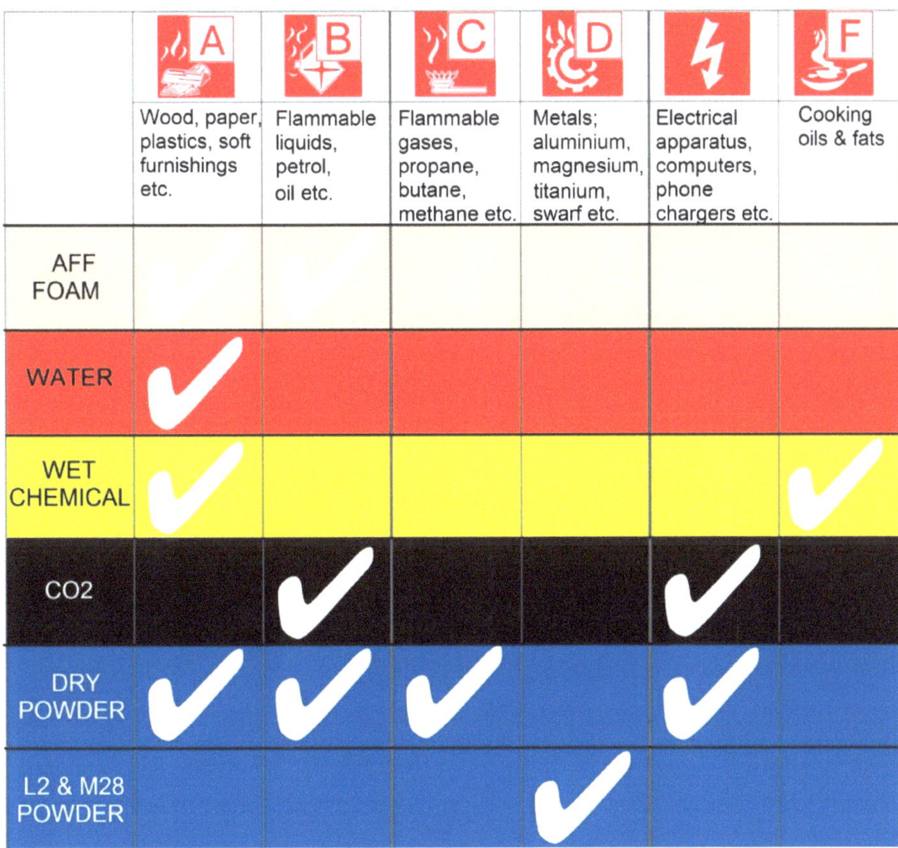

	A Wood, paper, plastics, soft furnishings etc.	B Flammable liquids, petrol, oil etc.	C Flammable gases, propane, butane, methane etc.	D Metals; aluminium, magnesium, titanium, swarf etc.	Electrical apparatus, computers, phone chargers etc.	F Cooking oils & fats
AFF FOAM						
WATER	✔					
WET CHEMICAL	✔					✔
CO2		✔			✔	
DRY POWDER	✔	✔	✔		✔	
L2 & M28 POWDER				✔		

Fire extinguishers are designed to tackle specific types of fire. There are six different classes of fire and several different types of fire extinguishers.

Classes of fire

- Class A - fires involving solid materials such as wood, paper or textiles.
- Class B - fires involving flammable liquids such as petrol, diesel or oils.
- Class C - fires involving gases.
- Class D - fires involving metals.
- Class E - fires involving live electrical apparatus. (Technically 'Class E' doesn't exists however this is used for convenience here)
- Class F - fires involving cooking oils such as in deep-fat

fryers

2.7 Types of Fire Extinguisher

1. Water extinguishers

Water extinguishers are one of the most cost-effective ways to fight Class A fires, those fueled by solid materials such as paper, wood and textiles.

There are four different types of water extinguishers: water jet, water spray, water with additives and water mist or fog.

- Water jet extinguishers work by spraying a jet of water at the burning materials, cooling them and preventing re-ignition. They should not be used on live electrical equipment.

- Water spray extinguishers use a very fine spray of water droplets, each droplet is surrounded by air which is non-conductive. Most water spray fire extinguishers carry a 35 kV dielectric test approval which means they have been tested on a 35,000 Volt electrical source at one meter.

- Water extinguishers with additives are water extinguishers with foaming chemicals added. The water loses its natural surface tension meaning that it can soak into the burning materials more effectively. Adding the chemicals to the water means that a smaller extinguisher can produce the same fire rating as a larger, water only extinguisher.

Water mist, or fog extinguishers apply water in the form of mist, or fog, the droplets are much smaller than those from the water spray extinguisher. The smaller the droplet, the larger its surface area in relation to its size, the quicker the droplet evaporates which absorbs the heat energy faster. The downside is the smaller the droplet the less it weighs and therefore the less powerful the cloud of water. All water extinguishers have a red label.

2. Foam extinguishers

Foam fire extinguishers can be used on Class A and B fires. They are most suited to extinguishing liquid fires such as petrol or diesel and are more versatile than water jet extinguishers because they can also be used on solids such as wood and paper. The foam extinguishes liquid fires by sealing the surface of the liquid, preventing flammable vapor reaching the air and starving the fire of fuel. They are not suitable for use on free flowing liquid fires. Foam extinguishers have a cream label.

3. Powder extinguishers

Powder extinguishers are a good multi-purpose fire extinguisher because they can be used on Class A, B and C fires. They can also be used on fires involving electrical equipment however, they do not cool the fire so it can re-ignite. Powder extinguishers can also create a loss of visibility and may create breathing problems. They are not generally recommended for use inside buildings unless there is absolutely no alternative. Powder extinguishers have a blue label.

4. Carbon dioxide extinguishers (CO2)

CO2 extinguishers are ideal for places with a lot of electrical equipment such as offices or server rooms because they are safe to use on fires involving electrical apparatus. Carbon dioxide extinguishers do not leave any residue, unlike a foam extinguisher. They can also be used on Class B fires, those involving flammable liquids such paraffin or petrol. CO2 extinguishers work by smothering the fire and cutting off the supply of air. Carbon Dioxide Extinguishers (CO2) have a black label.

5. Wet chemical extinguishers

Wet chemical extinguishers are suitable for use on Class F fires involving cooking oils and fats, such as lard, olive oil, sunflower oil, maize oil and butter. They are extremely effective, when used correctly. The wet chemical rapidly knocks the flames out, cools the burning oil and chemically reacts to form a soap-like solution, sealing the surface and preventing re-ignition. Although they are primarily designed for use on Class F fires, cooking oils and deep fat fryers. They can also be used on Class A fires (wood, paper and fabrics) and Class B fires (flammable liquids). B Wet chemical extinguishers have a yellow label.

6. Fire blankets

Fire blankets are primarily for use on hot oil fires such as frying pans or small deep fat fryers. They can also be used on someone whose clothing has caught fire. They work by smothering the fire, stopping access to the oxygen fueling it and extinguishing it.

Fire extinguishers are marked with letters and symbols that indicate the types of fire they can extinguish. It is critically important to understand the types and appropriate uses. Fires can actually grow if you use a wrong extinguisher. If the fire requires a solution or liquid that could act as a conductor, all electrical equipment must be de-energized. Prevention, compliance to procedures, regular inspections and knowledge of potential fire hazards can help prevent accident. Employee need to be trained on hazards of fire and hoe to operate fire extinguisher while working a highly inflammable environment.

There is an acronym (PASS) to remember for better use of fire extinguisher

P: pull the pin of the extinguisher

A: aim at the base of the fire

S: squeeze the handle of the extinguisher

S: swipe from side to side.

CHAPTER 3

PREPARING AGAINST HAZARDS AT WORKPLACE

3.1 Preparing Against Hazards at Workplace

A safety conscious worker should know the reason for working, what level of risk should be taken, who will be affected if the worker takes a risk and gets injured, what should be done to prevent injury at workplace and home, can the worker make a mistake even with years of experience, it's important that a worker goes home safe to your family and return to work the same way.

As we all know some work environments involves some hazards that could become life threatening, therefore every worker should be able to:

1. Recognize, evaluate and control hazards

2. Lists several types of PPEs

3. Determine what safety equipment to use

4. Identify general safe practices for tool and equipment use.

3.2 Personal Protective Equipment (PPE)

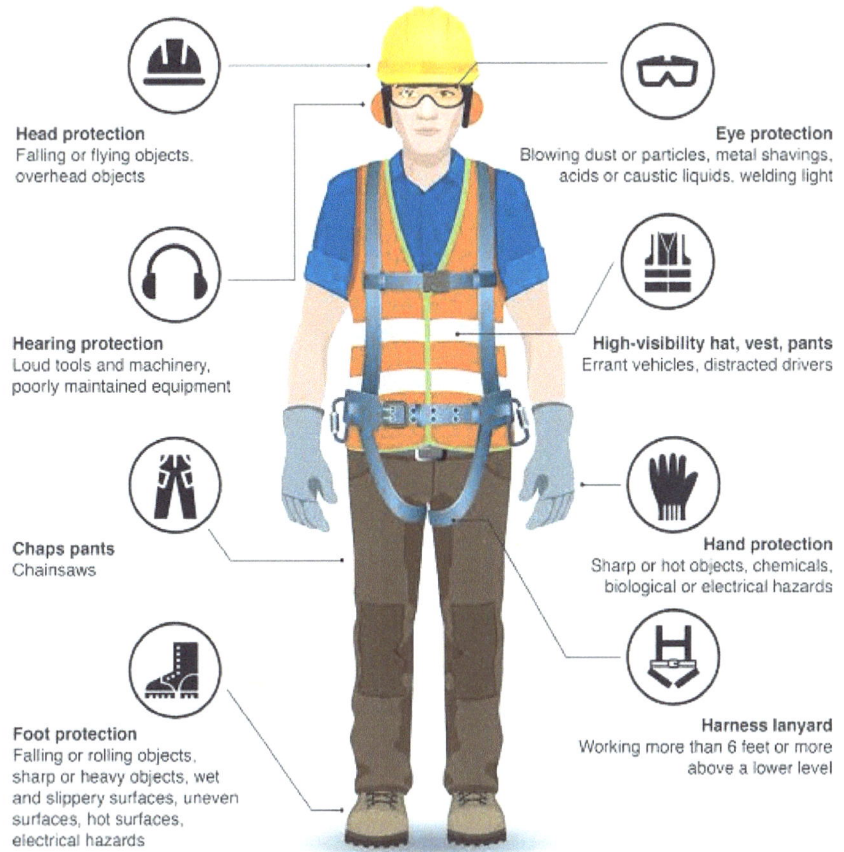

Personal protective equipment is a protective clothing, helmet, goggles or other garment or equipment designed to protect the wearer's body from injury or infection. Physical, electrical, chemicals, biohazards and airborne particles are addressed by PPE. It is the responsibility of the worker to use equipment properly after being trained on a proper fit and use. Electrical protective gloves with high electrical resistance, fire resistant clothing and fall arrester (Lanyard) are among the most important articles or personal protection for electrical workers. Electrical protective gloves are categorized by the level of voltage protection they provide and whether they are resistant to ozone as follows:

Class Zero: 1000v – 5000vAC max

Class One: 7,500v – 10,000vAC

Class Two: 10,000 – 20,000vAC

Class Three: 20000 – 30000vAC

Class Four: 30000 – 40000Vac

Employers must teach employees how to use and care for their protectors and supervise them on the job to ensure they continue to wear them correctly.

3.3 Helmet Colours and Meanings

Colour		Meaning
Yellow		Labourer, Heavy-duty operations, & Construction tasks
Grey		Site visitors
Red		Firefighters
Brown		Welders, high heat operations
Blue		Electricians and Technical operators
Green		Safety officers
Pink		female workers* *in some companies it is used as an additional helmet
White		Managers, Engineers, Supervisors, Foreman

Hundreds of types of tools and equipment are used on daily basis by large number of workers. Workers must remember that deviation from appropriate and safe use protocol can cause serious injuries or death. Workers are responsible for following the guideline and procedures of the tooling equipment manuals. They outline safe and proper usage and vital information. Employers are responsible for providing safety programs, meetings and toolbox talks to communicate current or potential hazards to worker before start of work. Compliance with safety training programs including discussions regarding tool and equipment use help to ensure a safe and hazard-free workplace.

3.4 Near Misses

Near misses are unwanted events which under different circumstances would have resulted in injury

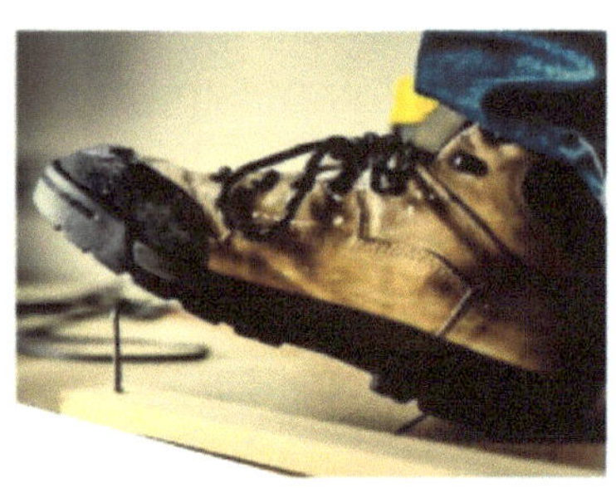

Accident in an organization have many negative effects not only to the damage it causes to the employees, assets, and environment but it dents the company's reputation in many ways. To maintain a safe and healthy working environment, a company must implement strong HSE standards/principles that are well anchored in the organizational Code of Conduct. HSE principles must be highly prioritized by the management and all concerned, informing the need to maintain high standards of HSE, encompassing personnels from Strategic, Tactical and Operational management

Elements Of A Successful HSE Management System

1. Safety Inspection Checklist

2. The control and distribution of up-to-date documents

3. Risk Assessment

4.   Follow up laws on Health, Safety and Environment regulations for compliance

5. Establish experienced HSE Team

6. Measurable performance metrics

7. Organizing regular meetings and communication strategy

8. Organizing regular management reviews

9. Ensure Internal Auditing Policy and Schedule

10. Organizing Training program for the workforce

11. Organizing Emergency Response Plan

Causes Of Health And Safety Hazards While Working

Health and safety hazard don't occur because of a single event, accident is always associated with multiple factors that result in those unfortunate events and its pertinent for employers to be aware of such factors as this will help reduce accident in workplace.

The following can cause harm or death to lives and properties; Height, Sharp objects, Slippery floor, Unlabeled materials, Material obstruction, Horseplay (Unwanted Joke), Desperation while working etc.

3.5 Injury Preventive Measures While Working

Ensure You Protect Yourself Against Falling From Height By Adopting Best International Practices

While Working At Heights (WAHs) above 6ft, ensure that you erect a temporary platform (Ladder or Scaffold.

Stop Work When It Is Raining

It's high risk practice to carry on installation while it is raining especially when power is concern. Ensure that all power system installation work stop while it's raining because even if you are working in the power house, thunder strike can cause a serious damage to you or the equipment

Ensure You Avoid Electric Shock By All Means

There are many ways to guide against being electrocuted while working on any power system installation project. The use of PPE is a step in the right direction, don't work with your bare hands and ensure that the tools you are using are appropriate for the job at hand. The tools below can't be used to work on electrical circuit because they are not properly insulated. Ensure the metal tools are well insulated before working on electrical circuits. Proper use and regular maintenance of the work tools must be given due consideration.

Don't Work Alone

Working alone is not only risky when working in any power project but the same applies when working on other project that is not in the power generation business. Accident may occur anytime while you are working on any project and if you don't have someone to rescue you, the damage will be much compared to when you are in a desperate situation and you have someone available to render help to you.

Barricade The Work Area While Working At Height.

Signs and barricades are used whenever a potential hazard is present in a work area. Don't disregard those signs.

Use Lanyard Tool To Tie Off Tools While Carrying Tools

Ensure The Right Working Tools Are Used During power system Installation.

As a professional, you must have your work tools

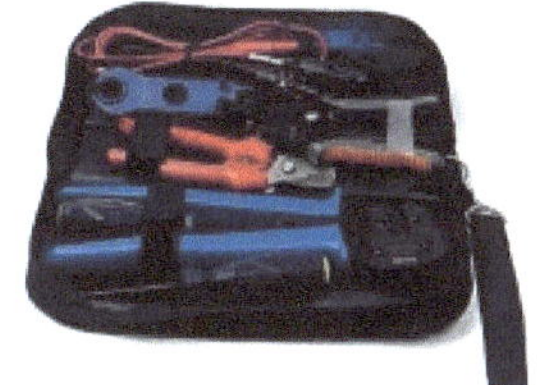

Check For Damage Tools And Replace Them

Working with damage tools is a total no especially in the power generation business, it slows down the whole process and it's a big threat to the safety of lives and property.

Scaffold Checklist

Scaffold is basically used during solar panel installation. Don't erect scaffold yourself because you lack the requisite qualification. All scaffold use on site must have the

following:

> A work permit before erection

> A completed scaffolding checklist

> A scaffold fit for use inspection label attach to it before you climb it

SCAFFOLD INSPECTION CHECKLIST

Company Name:	Scaffold Location:		
Completed by:	Time: Date:		

SAFETY CHECKS	Yes	No	Comments
Scaffold components, planking/decking in good condition? Planks graded for scaffold?			
All scaffold components in place and no defects?			
Competent person in charge of erection/inspection?			
Mud Sills properly placed and adequate sized when required?			
Screw jacks being used to level and plumb scaffold when required?			
Base plates and/or screw jacks in firm contact with mudsills and frame?			
Scaffold is level and plumb?			
Scaffold legs braced, with braces properly attached?			
Guard railing in place on all open sides and ends?			
Visual check to verify clamps secured in place?			
Scaffold secured to structure to prevent movement?			
Brackets, tube and clamp, and accessories properly placed with wedges tightened?			
Area around scaffold has been secured/roped off?			
Planks have minimum 12" overlap and extend 6" beyond supports?			
Toe boards properly installed when required?			
Proper access to get on and off the scaffold? Ladder secured in place?			
Scaffold control tag has been signed and approved for use?			
If inspection reveals scaffold is unsafe to use, has "Do Not Use" tag been placed at all access points?			
Signature:			

Safety Measures During Excavation

> Ensure you barricade the work area

> Carryout trail test. Ensure you dig slowly. The first two feet must be dig gradually so that you don't cut any cable that was buried on the ground for another purpose.

> Don't undermine nearby structures, dig away from nearby structures and always use safe digging practices

> Excavation must be checked every day before the commencement of work and after any event that may affect the stability of the excavation.

> An access to the excavation and out of the excavation must be provided

Safety Measures While Working In The Power House

> Fire extinguisher is one basic necessity in any power house during system installation. Fire Extinguisher should be part of the basic needs in any facility. Fire outbreak occurs in any facilities during or after installations.

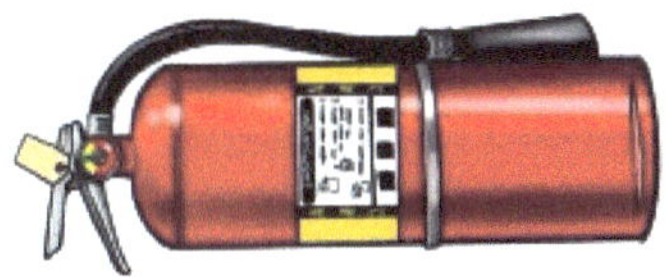

> Ensure all your work tools are properly insulated. Using metal tools to work on electrical circuit is a serious threat to life. Ensure that all metal part of any tool use in electrical circuit is properly insulated.

> Cables and battery terminals must be professionally terminated. Ensure you don't use manual method to lock cables or battery terminals. Improper termination of cable is one of the reason we have fire outbreak in some installation sites

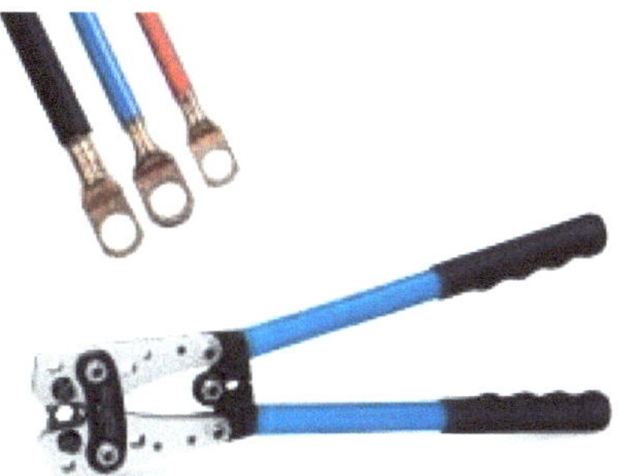

> Earthing all the components is a must during any system installation

> Before connecting any component, polarity check must be done.

> Accident can occur due to obstruction on site and it's important that house-keeping is carried out at the close of work everyday

> There must be professional **cable management practices, cable arrangement, Labelling and Concealing cables** inside the trunk during power system installation

> All the power components must be properly earth

> The right size of cable is key to the success of any power system and using the wrong size of cable will cause voltage drop or fire outbreak down the road that could make the area unsafe.

ENSURE YOU GET THE PDF MATERIAL ATTACHED TO THIS TEXTBOOK ON JOB HAZARD

ASSESSMENT, ACTIVITIES, POTENTIAL HAZARDS AND SAFETY MEASURES THAT IS ASSOCIATED WITH SUCH PRODUCT AND ACTIVITY

It's assumed that there is always risk of accident (hazard) associated with any filed of human endeavor. Going by this, being safety conscious and the ability to manage hazards is key to a successful day to day running of our businesses, home and in our workplaces. In our environments, we can be exposed to different levels of hazard while working which include;

Unsafe Acts or unsafe condition

Near Misses

Minor Accident (First Aid)

Serious Accident

Fatality

For the safety of lives and properties, you must always learn to work on **Safe Condition**, we should not even try working on an unsafe condition let alone working in the Near Misses condition. Going to the level of near misses is dangerous

CHAPTER 4
SAFETY ADMINISTRATION AND POLICIES

Safety Policies And Standards

4.1 Safety Policies

Companies are required to document and provide a site wise

safety plan. A safety plan describes the

process for identifying physical and health hazards that could harm workers, procedure to prevent

accidents and steps to take when accidents occur. The basic elements include

A goal statement.

Hazard identification.

Hazard control and safe practices.

Emergency and accident response.

Employee training and communication.

Record keeping.

There are many regulations and many levels of government and non-government agencies contributing

to maintaining safety and emergency responses. The utility sector being large and diverse has no single

entity responsible for all safety regulations. In addition to federal agencies and industry groups, there

are also many state and local agencies that enforce safe and secure operation for the protection of people,

data, environment, property and institutions.

4.2 Environmental Policies

The public is becoming aware of the possibility of negative impacts on our environment caused by

industrial activities. All levels of governing body have contributed to the creation of environmental

regulations to mitigate environmental pollution.

In addition to government imposed regulations upon energy and utility companies, some companies

created and enforced additional environmental policies to further protect the environment, health and

safety of employees, customers, and general public. These policies includes:

Compliance: this indicates you are operating in accordance with the applicable environmental health and safety laws and regulations and other standard to the company.

Risk reduction: the public is utilizing facility layout and operation protocols

Improved performance: the public is conducting periodic environmental health and safety valuations

and continuously improving operations and management systems.

Corrective action: the public promptly correct unsafe conditions.

Pollution prevention: the public efforts are focused on minimizing waste, promote recycling & reuse

and disposing of waste using methods.

Resource conservation: the public is taking into account the conservation of natural resources,

improvements in energy efficiency and use of sustainable energy resources.

Employee awareness: the employer informs, trains and motivates employees to carry out their

responsibility in a safe and environmental friendly manner

Public awareness: the public is made aware of policies and inform customers, neighbors and

appropriate government officials of any significant environmental, health or safety aspects of the

operations in time.

4.3 Community Safety Legislation

Several agencies and governing bodies are entrusted with maintaining environmental regulations that affect the utility and energy industry which includes:

Clean Water Act: this governs pollution of our nation's waters, water discharges from electric power generation facilities are regulated by this act.

Clean Air Act: this governs air quality through the reduction of smog and air pollution, regulations of

ambient Air Quality Standard (AQS) of a particular area, this doesn't affect the electric power generating industry.

Clean Air Power Initiatives: this Act was initiated to improve air pollution efforts within the electric

power generating industry and regulate the three major pollutants emitted by electric power generators

(SO2, NOX and Mercury)

Hazardous Materials Transportation Act: this act regulates the transportation of hazardous materials including radioactive materials.

Atomic Energy Act: this regulates the management of nuclear materials and nuclear facilities. Emergency Planning and Right to Know Act: this supports emergency planning efforts at different levels of government.

4.4 OSHA and HSE Policies/Standards

Occupational Safety & Health Act (OSHA) and Health, Safety & Environment (HSE) regulations were signed into law to protect employer and employee. These standards and its agencies enforce workplace safety and health standards, conduct research on occupational safety and health, and arbitrate enforcement actions challenged by employers. OSHA and HSE standards establish requirement designed to protect employees against workplace hazards.

OSHA safety standards are intended to protect against traumatic injury while

HSE safety standards are designed to address potential exposure to harmful substances and possible illness.

4.5 Company Safety Policies and Worker's Rights

Workers' Right in the Workplace:

As an employee, a worker can receive training from employer as required by OSHA standards. A worker

may request information from employer about OSHA standards, worker's injuries, illness, job hazards, workers' right and request action from employer to correct hazards or violations.

A worker has the right to file a complaint with OSHA if the worker believes there are violations of OSHA standards or serious workplace hazards and may be involved in OSHA inspection and result of the workplace.

Employer's Right in the Workplace:

Employer has right as well and may receive compliance assistance from OSHA, get involved in OSHA inspection, find out result of the OSHA inspection of the workplace and enforce workers compliance with OSHA and HSE standards.

OSHA has general regulation that contain several sections and subparts pertinent to electrical work. These includes:

General electrical practice.

Electrical safety standards and practical safeguarding of workers.

Design safety standards related to work practices.

Safety related maintenance requirements.

Safety requirements for special equipment.

Personal Protective Equipment (PPEs)

General environmental control

OSHA determines that there was a risk to health and safety of workers in the electrical power generation, transmission and distribution due their exposure to electrical hazards and hence updates the regulations for general electrical industry.

New OSHA standards includes requirements relating to training, job briefings, confined space, hazardous energy control, working on or near energized parts, live-line tools, grounding for employees protection,

working on underground and overhead installations, line-clearance tree trimming, work in substations

and generating plants, other special conditions and equipment unique to generation, transmission and distribution.

Compliance with these regulations is mandated by OSHA to prevent injuries to employees working with electrical power systems.

An Employee Handbook: a great tool of company-wide communication used to convey the following:

Rules and guidelines, Employer expectation, Policies, Consequences for violation, Commitment to fair

and equal treatment, Culture of safety, Fairness and Integrity.

Employees have the right to review the log/record of work-related injuries and illness that result in death,

days away from work, restricted work activity or job transfer, medical treatment beyond first aid and loss

of consciousness. Employers must record and post summary of work-related injuries and illness in a visible location in compliance with OSHA standards.

OSHA is authorized to conduct workplace inspections that determine compliance with safe healthful

workplace practices and review lockout tag, emergency and fire plans, respiratory protection plans, hearing conservation programs, materials safety data sheets and make safety checklist a part of safety program.

It is imperative for all levels of employees to be consistent and execute safety and health enforcement.

Everyone is accountable for workplace safety.

4.6 Good Work-Life Balance

A healthy work-life balance will mean different things to us all. It's not so much about splitting your

time 50/50 between work and leisure but making sure you feel fulfilled and content in both areas of
your life. A healthy balance could be:

- Meeting your deadlines at work while still having time for friends and hobbies
- Having enough time to sleep properly and eat well
- Not worrying about work when you're at home.

This can be challenging if, for example, we also have caring responsibilities, a demanding boss or
health difficulties.

How do I know if my work-life balance is unhealthy ?

It can be easy to normalize working long hours or being under extreme stress, especially if we've been doing it for a long time or all our colleagues are in the same boat. Our assumptions and habits around work can become deep-rooted unless we take a step back once in a while.

It's not always possible to make changes at work: if you're on a zero-hours contract, you might not
feel comfortable speaking up, for instance, or you might need to work long hours to earn enough
money to pay your bills. But for those who can make changes, recent research suggests regularly
checking your work-life balance by following five steps.

1. **Pause.** Ask yourself: what's currently causing me stress or unhappiness? How is that affecting my work and personal life? What am I prioritizing? What am I losing out on? We often don't take the time to reflect on work until there's a major life event, such as the birth of a child or the loss of someone close to us. But just pausing and thinking about your priorities can help you discover whether the way you're living and working is right for you

2. **Pay attention to your feelings.** Now you're more aware of your current situation, how does it make you feel? Are you fulfilled and happy or angry and resentful? Being aware of your feelings can help you decide which

changes you want to make

3. **Reprioritize.** Think about what needs to change. For example, you might want to ask yourself if working long hours is worth losing out on family time or whether working weekends is worth losing out on your social life

4. **Consider your alternatives.** Is there anything at work you can change to meet your new priorities?

5. **Make changes.** Maybe asking for flexible hours, making sure you use all your annual leave or not checking your emails at the weekend.

Helping Yourself

There are steps you can take to improve your work-life balance. It can be difficult or impossible to stand up for yourself at work if you're precariously employed or worried about losing your job. Make sure you know your rights (see below) and see if any of these tips are safe for you to try.

- Understand your rights at work. Citizens Advice has information on contracts, working hours, sick pay, parental leave and more. For example, if you have a disability (which can include mental and physical conditions), your employer might have a duty to make reasonable adjustments. This could include changes to your working hours.

- Speak up when the expectations and demands of work are too much. Your manager and employer need to know where the pressures lie in order to address them.

- Try to 'work smart, not long'. This involves prioritizing - allowing yourself a certain amount of time per task - and trying not to get caught up in less productive activities such as unstructured meetings.

- Take proper breaks at work. For example, take at least half an hour for lunch and get out of the workplace if you can. You're legally entitled to certain breaks during the day and working week

- Try to draw a line between work and home. If you work from home, try to keep to a routine, make a dedicated workspace and switch off when the working day is over.

- Work-related stress can seriously affect your mental health. Our page on stress has ideas to reduce it, for example, through exercise, eating well or supportive friendships.

- If work makes you feel you don't have quality time for your partner or friends, read articles on realigning your work-life balance. They include scheduling time together, getting help with chores and childcare and making every second count if you don't have much spare time.

- Keep track of your working hours over weeks or months rather than days. This will give you a better picture of your work-life balance. Factor in hours spent worrying or thinking about work too.

they're a good indicator of work-related stress. If possible, assess your work-life balance with your colleagues and management staff. The more visible the process, the more likely it is to have an effect.

How Your Workplace Can Help

Finding a balance shouldn't just be down to you. Your manager and workplace also play a role. They should:

- Encourage a culture of openness so you can speak up if you're under too much pressure train managers to spot stress and poor work-life balance

- Offer flexible and remote working where possible encourage breaks, whether that's during the working day or by using annual leave

- Regularly review your workload to make sure it's achievable give you time off to volunteer

- Increase support for parents and carers, so they're not forced to leave

- Allow you to attend counselling and support services during working hours as they would for other medical appointments

- Encourage stress-relieving activities such as lunchtime exercise or relaxation classes ask employees what would improve their work-life balance

4.7 Healthy Lifestyle

10 Tips For Maintaining A Healthy Lifestyle

In recent times we began working from home away from workplaces, and keeping social distance for as many people as possible. As we stay home and are stuck with the foods that have been in our fridge or pastry for a while, we are temporarily living a sedentary lifestyle with increased odds of physical inactivity, excessive eating and sitting, stress, anxiety and depression. Many of people will gain some weight and other health problems. Therefore, the following health tips are recommended;

Measure and Watch Your Weight
Keeping track of your body weight on a daily or weekly basis will help you see what you're losing and/or

what you're gaining.

Limit Unhealthy Foods and Eat Healthy Meals.

Do not forget to eat breakfast and choose a nutritious meal with more protein and fiber and less fat, sugar,

and calories. Research for more information on weight-control foods and dietary recommendations

Take Multivitamin Supplements

To make sure you have sufficient levels of nutrients, taking a daily multivitamin supplement is a good idea, especially when you do not have a variety of vegetables and fruits at home. Many micronutrients are vital to your immune system, including vitamins A, B6, B12, C, D, and E, as well as zinc, iron, copper, selenium, and magnesium. However, there's currently no available evidence that adding any supplements or "miracle mineral supplements" to your diet will help protect you from the virus or increase recovery. In some cases,

high doses of vitamins can be bad for your health.

Drink Water and Stay Hydrated, and Limit Sugared Beverages

Drink water regularly to stay healthy, but there is no evidence that drinking water frequently (e.g. every 15 minutes) can help prevent any viral infection.

Exercise Regularly and Be Physically Active

At this time, at-home workouts may be a good idea. But you can also walk your dog or run outside. Be sure you know what's going on in your area and if there are any restrictions or mandatory self-quarantines.

Reduce Sitting and Screen Time

Exercise can't immunize you from your sedentary time. Even people who exercise regularly could be at increased risk for diabetes and heart disease and stroke if they spend lots of time sitting behind computers. Practically speaking, you could consider taking breaks from sedentary time, such as walking around the office/room a couple of times in a day.

Get Enough Good Sleep

There is a very strong connection between sleep quality and quantity and your immune system. You can

keep your immune system functioning properly by getting seven to eight hours of sleep each night

Go Easy on Alcohol and Stay Sober

Drinking alcohol does not protect you from the coronavirus infection. Don't forget that those alcohol

calories can add up quickly. Alcohol should always be consumed in moderation

Find Ways to Manage Your Emotions

It is common for people to have feelings of fear, anxiety, sadness, and uncertainty during a pandemic.

To minimize stress-related weight gain.

ABOUT THE AUTHOR

Victor Chinaza Okereke

The author is a safety (HSE) professional with years of career experience in electrical engineering and labour sector. He has authored many professional textbooks having acquired vast field experience, academic qualifications, professional certifications, leadership positions and several awards from reputable organizations/institutions; University At Buffalo, The State University of New York. By successfully bringing a real world experience into this book using best research methodology and professional practices, all these are with the view to improving and sharpening the HSE awareness of the user

www.ingramcontent.com/pod-product-compliance
Lightning Source LLC
Chambersburg PA
CBHW040302240726
48664CB00006B/1347